THUNDEROUS MIRACLE

&

DELIVERANCE PRAYER BOOK

Evangelist Chidinma Anokwute

WARNING!

This deliverance prayer book is not meant to take away your faith, which is in Christ Jesus or to undermine your God-given spiritual gift, neither a substitute for the Holy Bible. The prayers in this book are revelations, **given** by the Holy Spirit and not for magical purposes.
This prayer book **destroys satanic strategies and defeats the enemies of your life.**

Pay attention to follow strictly the steps for fasting and be in the spirit during the prayers for fast result.

Lord Jesus, I ask for angelic help for the readers of this book.

DEDICATION

This book is dedicated first to God Almighty through his son Jesus Christ who gave me the power, strength, wisdom and inspiration throughout the writing of this book.

PREFACE

The Holy Spirit mandated me to write these deliverance prayers. I heard the voice of God telling me about the power of Thunder, and this was my first time to reflect on Thunder as a tool and weapon used by God to end strongholds and the same time bring his power to act on earth. This voice was sounding continuously on my left ear for over Three (3) weeks saying, "Write what I will tell you". Then as soon as I started writing the book, the Lord said to me "Spread the word, and let my people get delivered through this book". By the grace of God, this book contains over 300 prayer points, arranged to inspire and guide you to your deliverance.

My special thanks go to our Lord Jesus Christ and the Holy Spirit, for divine direction, wisdom, guidance and divine revelation throughout the writing of this book.

I sincerely thank my husband Mr. Constantius Anokwute for his encouragement and moral support. I also wish to express my gratitude to Mrs. Joy Anikwe, my prayer partner and kingdom builder, for her encouragement and Minister Theddeues & Mrs. Ifeoma Onwumere for their prayers and support in ministry.

Finally, I am grateful to Hon. Ndukwu Oguibe of 4Him Publications, for his professional guidance.

Evangelist Chidinma Anokwute

CONTENTS

1

Introduction

The thunderous miracle prayer book is God's revelational and spirit-filled deliverance prayer book that provides divine help to people confronted with diverse spiritual attacks and re-occurring intractable life problems. In our societies today, so many people are consciously or unconsciously living in one bondage or the other, a consequence of either personal or parental dedication to altars which are foundational. Some of these foundational forms of bondage include ancestral bondage, community-associated bondage, Church-related bondage, occultic bondage and voice bondage. Good knowledge of each of these is necessary for dealing with certain issues in life. However, our attention in this book will focus on voice bondage, with the view to exposing some satanic strategies, and prayers that will destroy powers of darkness and set the captive free.

Voice Bondage

This experience occurs often when a person hears strange words in a solitary state, or in a crowd with people, which overpowers the sanity of the person's mind and eliminates rationality. Many prophets in the bible heard the voice of God and obeyed and carried out his instructions while some prophets disobeyed the voice of God. Prophet Ezekiel "heard a voice of one that spoke" (Ezekiel 2:2). Elijah understood the voice he heard was from God as it came in a gentle whisper (1 King 19:11-14). The voice said to Elijah what are you doing here? Elijah explained himself to God and carried out the instructions as commanded by the spirit of God. Throughout the old testaments, the voice of God was a communication tool used to oversee the affairs of Israel. Most of the prophets disobeyed the voice of God and entered into bondages which crippled their calling. For example, Jonah was a prophet of God who disobeyed God by refusing to go to Nineveh and he was swallowed by fish and the mercies of God brought Jonah out of the belly of the fish. Most people in this present age are controlled by negative voices that kill the sanity of the society.

Majority of the teens hear the voice of death and are bound with fear. They will not tell anyone or know anyone who could be of help to them. Many of them end up committing suicide. Presently, Europe, America and other parts of the world are in distress as a result of an increase in the rate of suicide. Some people hear voices asking them not to eat proper food; some hear voices telling them to rape; some hear voices telling them to steal, smoke etc.

Many voices are out in the world to depopulate the kingdom of God, but the bible says in John 10: 27-28, "*My sheep hear my voice, and I know them and they follow me: And I give unto them eternal life, and they shall never perish, neither shall any man pluck them out of my Hand.*"

The voice of God is goodness, truth, mercy, deliverance, wisdom and protection to his people. **The voice of God has a positive impact in the lives of those who hear it. To the believer in Christ, the voice of God takes him captive and constrains him to do what is good always. It compels the believer to be bound to God's will. In this sense, voice bondage can be a positive experience as Paul severally refers to himself as "a prisoner of Christ" totally and completely sold to His will.** Eph 3:1; Eph 4:1; Philemon 1:1,9,23

Reject Negative Voice

Discovery is the process of obtaining information and it does wake people's consciousness. After reading this piece of information about voice, it will help you to assess and re-assess your thoughts, the voices you have heard in solitary situations, voices that speak over your life or situations which keep you uncomfortable. Don't fail to assess your actions while hearing the negative voices. I will like you to start from today to document voices that are strange to you which you have encountered while you are alone or in the public. Also write down negative voices that usually come over your head when you are in distress, or alone. Use the word of God in 2 Corinthians 10:5 "Casting down imaginations, and every high thing that exalteth itself against the knowledge of God, and bringing into captivity every thought to the obedience of Christ" to always cancel and reject every negative voice you've heard in the past whether in the dream or real life or even from your head, stand up in anger in your spirit to cancel the devilish voices. Don't give room to the devil to expand his business in your life.

Research has it that about 10% of people in the world have heard experiences of hearing voices at some point in their lives especially when they have problems that they cannot solve at a time (https://www.mentalhealth.org.uk/a-to-z/h/hearing-voices).   Jesus challenged Satan in Mathew 4:1-7, so you should also stand and challenge Satan yourself. You are created to do greater works according to John 14 v 12. God has given you the power to challenge your situation by voicing out the scripture over your condition, to destroy what looks like facts from the kingdom of darkness. Always confess positively no matter what you are going through. The prayers in this book will help you to obtain your desired breakthrough.

The Voice of God
The voice of God comes like thunder which strikes every situation, condition, powers, and laws that negatively affect your life on earth. Job 37:5 *"God thundered marvelously with His voice; great things doeth he, which we cannot comprehend."* Hearing the voice of God involves a deep commitment in God's word, working with the Holy Spirit, walking in faith, operating in Holiness, walking in righteousness, in God's love and peace. As a child of God, you need to keep up a continual relationship with Christ Jesus. For continuation in the service of the Lord Jesus brings freedom. When you are working in God's vineyard, relationship with Jesus is an unending process, it is a ceaseless, and unbroken relationship. No matter what life throws at you, don't break the relationship you have with Christ Jesus rather pursue to overtake.

David said in 1 Samuel 30:8,
> And David enquired at the Lord, saying,
> Shall I pursue after this troop? Shall I
> overtake them? And he answered him,
> pursue: for thou shalt surely overtake
> them, and without fail recover all. (KJV).

David was in the middle of a battle, he didn't give up, but he rather sought to hear the voice of God thunder in his case, to deliver him from the hands of Amalekites. David encouraged himself in the Lord his God. While you are in the wilderness, encourage yourself in the Lord; for sure that sickness will not swallow you; for sure that satanic torment and spiritual attacks will not swallow you and your calling; for sure you will become a mother of children; for sure your court case is settled; for sure you will get your documentation settled; for sure the evil and marine power dominating your life is broken in Jesus Mighty name, Amen. What else are you battling with; the Lord will surely give you victory in all areas of your life.
"And I am sure of this, that he who began a good work in you will bring it to completion at the day of Jesus Christ". (Philippians 1:6)

The day Jesus Christ means, the day God will thunder his voice in your case, that same day the battle will be won in your favour. The day of Jesus Christ is the day God steps into your space; it also signifies the day you receive a long-awaited answer to your prayers; the day you overtake your enemies; the day you receive Holy Ghost and become born-again; Hallelujah!

David was a man after God's heart and he faced series of battles in his lifetime, but his unending relationship with God gave him deliverance and victory over all his enemies.

Why did Jesus the Son of God face many battles? Because Jesus was chosen to fulfill God's work and plan on earth. You and I are also called for the work of God, that's why we are in constant spiritual battle against witchcraft attack, health issues, poverty, war, pandemic, famine, discrimination, racism, religious attack, divorce, and unbelief. Fear not for you will overtake! Be encouraged, *"For the Son of man is come to seek and to save that which was lost."* (Luke 19: 10)

Philippians 2: 8-11 (NKJV) says,
> And being found in appearance as a man, He (Jesus) humbled Himself and became obedient to the point of death, even the death at the cross.
> Therefore God also has highly exalted Him and given Him the name which is above every name, that at the name of Jesus every knee should bow, of those in heaven and of those on earth , and of those under the earth, that every tongue shall confess that Jesus Christ is lord, to the glory of the Father.

Jesus was tempted in many ways. In the book of Luke 4:1-14 , verse 1 says, *"And Jesus being full of the Holy Ghost returned from Jordan, and was led by the Spirit into the wilderness"*. If you are a spirit-filled Christian, temptations will always come your way, but what matters most is that you will overcome the tempter, Hallelujah.
Jesus prayed to his father in heaven from the start of his journey to the end, and voice of God thundered in many ways while Jesus was on earth.

John 12:27 – 30;

Now is my soul troubled; and what shall I say? Father, save me from this hour: but for this cause came I unto this hour. Father, glorify thy name. Then came there a voice from heaven, saying, I have both glorified it, and will glorify it again. The people, therefore, that stood by, and heard it, said that it thundered: others said, an angel spoke to him. Jesus answered and said, *"This voice came not because of me, but for your sakes"*.

God's voice will thunder in your case as you obey God's word and pray the prayers in this book, you will receive your healing breakthrough, financial breakthrough, foundational deliverance, and deliverance from spiritual attacks in Jesus name Amen.

2

STEPS TO OVERCOME THE TEMPTER

1. **Holiness**

Holiness is the nature and character of God. For any man to be holy, that man must keep God's law according to the scripture. Also, it means keeping the laws of the land or society that are consistent with the scripture. Holiness being the nature of Christ, must affect all areas of your life from your thoughts, actions, services, lifestyle, desires, worship, relationships, temperament, spirituality etc. "You must be holy because I am holy" (1 Peter 1:16). Have you asked yourself what are the rules for holiness? You need to have right standing with God, which means standing on God's word and commandment. You shall not do evil and you need to be filled with the Holy Spirit. When fear comes to dominate your life, stand on God's word and manifest the nature of Christ through faith.

Hebrew 12:14 says, "*Follow Peace with all men, and Holiness, without which no man shall see the lord*". In my personal experience about holiness, I understand that I do not need to compromise with issues confronting my obedience to God's word, promises and his commandment rather quit from anything that will contaminate God's holy word. The scripture says,

> Therefore, since we have these promises, dear friends, let us purify ourselves from everything that contaminates body and spirit, perfecting holiness out of reverence for God" (2 Corinthians 7:1).

Keeping your body holy by fleeing from sexual immorality is very important in the journey of the Christian race, sex outside marriage can be destructive both physically and spiritually. Sex introduces spirits to the body that never departs until one goes to the grave. Familiar spirits use the face of your ex-boy and ex-girlfriend, ex-husband and ex-wife including family members to unleash their spiritual attacks. Presently, many people coming to counseling are attacked in the dream with the face of their husband or their wife making love, only to realise in the morning that they are having sex with spirit.

We need to quit fear, doubt, backbiting, witchcraft, occultism, lies, sexual immorality, hatred, chanters of demonic prayers, stealing, stop pulling other people down, don't oppress the poor, help the needy, by all means, avoid masturbation, and avoid greediness or excessively desiring wealth, or peoples possession which does not belong to you. Consider Ananias and Sapphira in the book of Acts 5:1 -11 who sold a parcel of land and kept part of the money to himself, lied to the Holy Spirit that they brought all to God, eventually both of them died. This is to show you that holiness does not accept compromise.

Holiness encourages the development of intimacy with God (Daniel 1:8). Holiness makes us useful for God's purposes in the society, in the churches and our family (2 Timothy 2: 20-21). Holiness in the life of a believer brings deliverance, miracle, pleases God, and produces fruitful relationship with God (1Peter 2:9-10). For you to be holy, always follow God's word and depart from iniquity, always keep yourself holy not serving other god's, for example, man-made gods, like wooden images, rocks, forest and trees, some people have made God of heaven too small in their eyes because their prayers were not answered when they needed it most, they finally resort to god made by a man, serving images that cannot speak or hear. When you as a child of God involve yourself in such practices, you have defiled God's holiness. "Therefore, since we have these promises, dear friends, let us purify ourselves from everything that contaminates body and spirit, perfecting holiness out of reverence for God." (2 Corinthians 7:1)

2. **Be filled with God's word and speak God's word over the Tempter**

The word of God is given to us for knowledge, for exercising power, for teaching, for building our faith in Christ Jesus, to know his will, or for divine direction, and to commune with the Holy Spirit. You must study the word of God to show yourself approved.

God's word is the foundation for holiness, without God's word how would you know him? Romans 10 v 13-17,

> For whosoever, shall call upon the name of the Lord shall be saved. How then shall they call on him in whom they have not believed? And how shall they believe in him of whom they have not heard? And how shall they hear without a preacher? So, then faith cometh by hearing, and hearing by the word of God.

The word of God you know will drive away your fears, drive away your enemies and attract blessings from above. The bible simply made it clear in Hosea 4:6, "*My people are destroyed from lack of knowledge. Because you have rejected knowledge, I also reject you as my priests; because you have ignored the law of your God, I also will ignore your children*". That's why the bible says that the truth you know will set you free. The truth from God's word exposes the present-day mysteries by revelation once you are holy. God's word keeps you holy and separates you from sin and dangers. All you need to do is to speak God's word over your problems and speak blessings over your life on daily basis in the name of Jesus Christ.

3. **Be a Worshipper and a Dweller in God's Presence**
Being a worshiper gives you a deeper connection to God. Worship on its own gives children of God opportunity to attend higher realm in the spirit without struggling. Worship catapults you to greatness like the case of Paul and Silas in the book of Acts chapter 16. The prison keeper bowed down to Paul and Silas after their worship shook the foundation of the prison and the prison doors were opened without human intervention. God's power of prayer and worship opened the doors of the prison, Hallelujah!

Paul and Silas did not pay any money to be released from the prison, but the power of worship and prayer brought down the presence of God that shook the gate and laid open the doors breaking the chains and keys. Overcoming the tempter is easier if you have a relationship with Jesus.

This testimony is about what happened this year 2020 during the pandemic. A boy of nine years old was hawking fruits in a particular market in the eastern part of Nigeria. Any day he came to sell his fruit, he will be singing in the market and people will be looking at him. On this fateful day, he was singing mostly worship songs which they usually sang in their church, a passer-by spotted him and took a video of the young boy singing in the market and made it go viral on Facebook. As of the time of this write up, the state government gave him a scholarship and enrolled him in government house choir with the donation of food item to the family. This is pure deliverance from poverty, this boy has his education now paid to the level of his choice. This is the power of worship which cannot be compared to anything. David praised God all his life despite his enemies. The proper and appropriate worship God requires from us is to sacrifice our life to Christ all year round without backsliding, no matter what life throws at us. Romans 12:1 urges us "*… to offer your bodies as a living sacrifice,* *holy and pleasing to God - this is your true and proper worship"*. Worship automatically brings down God's presence and makes you dwell in his presence.

4. **Be Obedient to God's Word**

To obey God's word means doing what His word says we should do, through studying the Bible. Deuteronomy 5:33 says,

> But following exactly the way that the
> Lord, your God, commanded you that
> you may live and prosper, and may have
> a long life in the land which you are to
> possess.

You must be a doer of God's word. Follow the footsteps of Jesus as it is written and as you hear it by listening to the voice of God through the Holy Spirit. In 2Timothy 3:16, the Bible speaking of itself says, *"All Scripture is inspired by God and is useful to teach us what is true and to make us realize what is wrong in our lives. It corrects us when we are wrong and teaches us to do what is right"*. Obedience simply teaches us the application of God's word into our daily life without argument. Doing what the law says you should do is the best way to be a good citizen, same technique applies to Christians to follow God's commandment without argument. Always ask the Holy Spirit to help you to walk in conformity with the standard of the Holy Scripture, by so doing, you will see yourself manifesting the greatness of God in your life, walking in righteousness, love, and living a blessed life.

Let me share this testimony with you here. I was praying one day, the Lord told me that as soon as I receive the money Government was owing me that I should give $1/4$ of the total money to the church building. I did as God told me in confirmation of the scripture in Proverbs 3:1, 9 and 10,

> My son, forget not my law; but let thine
> heart keep my commandments:
> Honour the Lord with thy substance, and
> with the first fruits of all thine increase:
> So shall thy barns be filled with plenty,
> and thy presses shall burst out with new
> wine.

After obeying the word of God, I got married to my desired husband, many doors opened to me in the same year. Glory be to God for walking in obedience to his word.

Again in obedience to the word of God in Hebrews 13:4 which says *"Marriage should be honoured by all, and the marriage bed kept pure, for God will judge the adulterer and all the sexually immoral"*. I told my husband that I will not sleep with her until my bride price is paid. As I obeyed the word all things worked out well as planned to God be the Glory.

5. **Be a Cheerful Giver**
A lot of people have wasted their God-given opportunity and success due to stinginess.

One day, while I was in the office, a colleague walked up to me telling me how his giving has skyrocketed him from ordinary banking officer to Head of Marketing in the branch. This colleague of mine is a tither and a cheerful giver in his local church. One day, he went to church, during the time of seed sowing and offering, the pastor said; who can sow a suit and clothes to young missionaries in the field? This colleague of mine donated the suit he wore to church, including his costly watch, necklace and his shoes. When he came to the office the following morning, he started narrating all that happened in the church to me, I looked at him as a foolish man thinking he has excess money but unknown to me, he was building his ladder of greatness. Today as I am writing this book, he has risen from marketing manager to branch manager. As if that was not enough, he was appointed the Commissioner for Finance in his state and at the end of his tenure, God gave him favour and he was elected a member of the Federal House of Representative in his constituency. This testimony of my former colleague taught me a great lesson. Never give God stupid, valueless seeds and offering because what you sow you will reap. Cain's gift was offensive to God and Cain reaped Curses.

Proverbs 21:27 says, *"The sacrifice of the wicked is abomination: how much more, when he bringeth it with a wicked mind"*

In 2 Corinthians 9:6-8, the Bible says,
> Each of you should give what you have decided in your heart to give, not reluctantly or under compulsion, for God loves a cheerful giver. And God is able to bless you abundantly, so that in all things at all times, having all that you need, you will abound in every good work.

The unique power of giving should not be underestimated, it touches the heart of God. Whenever man receives a gift, there is a burst of laughter that comes deep from his heart so does our God because we were created in his image. I pray that God will empower you to sow bountifully into God's work in Jesus name Amen.

6. **Do not be Ashamed to put your hope in Christ**
Apostle Paul speaking in Romans 1:16, said, "*I am not ashamed of the Gospel of our Lord Jesus Christ...*" The gospel of our Lord Jesus and entire scriptures give us freedom, information and spiritual knowledge of how to be great in life. When I was in my 20's I always meditated on the word of God, confessing I am the head and not the tail as written in the book of Deuteronomy 28:13. When I eventually finished my university degree I found out that my confession about greatness was not in vain rather it was an opportunity to spread the gospel of our Lord Jesus Christ. Psalms 68:11 says, "*The Lord gave the word: great was the company of those that published it.*"

Do not doubt your trust and hope in the Lord; always believe in his word without shame and doubt. When you look at the world today, the only place you will find peace and rest is in the lord. God's word as written in the Holy Bible is the perfect book that will give you greatness, peace and power to overcome the tempter.

7. **Ask God to Fill and Re-fill you with the Holy Spirit**. (Acts 2:3-4)
Ask God to fill you with the Holy Spirit. Man cannot give out the Holy Spirit to man except empowered by Jesus Christ and his father. I do not give as the world gives says the Lord in John 14:27a. The Holy Spirit exposes us to the hidden things of the Lord and of the world, and more importantly, how to move forward in life, and live above mediocrity. John 14:26,

> But the Comforter, which is the Holy Ghost, whom the Father will send in my name, he shall teach you all things, and bring all things to your remembrance, whatsoever I have said unto you.

In the world today, we compete for everything no matter the profession. For you to stand out, you need the Holy Spirit to show you the hidden things you do not understand or have knowledge of.

This testimony will shock you: When I was in Nigeria working as a contract staff in the bank, it came to a point when my contract on the job as a Customer Relation Officer was about to end and the head office said there is no renewal as they are employing experienced bankers. I wrote to the manager to recommend me for permanent position, but it happened that the head office is not recruiting internally. Then in the last month of my contract, I heard a voice during my routine night vigil saying "although your contract may have finished, but stay in the job, whether approved or not, for your permanent position". I turned to see who was talking to me but there was nobody in my room at that time and I immediately knew it was the voice of the Holy Spirit. On the last day of my contract, I walked up to the manager and said to him, I will be happy to stay here working while waiting for the head office to approve my permanent employment. The manager said that, it was at my own risk, as no one is responsible to pay my salary, but I can have a free lunch. I thanked the manager because the Holy Spirit never lies. I prayed day and night for a successful outcome of my application with constant fasting and prayer. After eight months of working without salary, the head office sent me a congratulatory letter saying, we are delighted to give you a permanent position in our bank and will keep you in the same branch. I was so happy and thanked God for speaking to me during my prayer in the power of the Holy Spirit. The voice of the Holy Spirit that I heard was what brought my greatness and gave me the job among people with higher professional banking experience. It is important as a Christian to be filled with the Holy Spirit which gives peace to a troubled soul. I tell you when you achieve greatness through the Holy Spirit, you will have peace of mind which comes from Christ Jesus. John 14:27 says, "*Peace I leave with you, my peace I give unto you: not as the world giveth, give I unto you. Let not your heart be troubled, neither let it be afraid*." Shalom.

Finally, always ask God in prayer to fill you with the Holy Spirit. The book of Matthew 7:7 says, "*Ask, it will be given to you…*" The Holy Spirit is that part of the father that hastens our communication and request. Acts 2:33 says,

> Therefore being by the right hand of God exalted, and having received of the Father the promise of the Holy Ghost, he hath shed forth this, which ye now see and hear.

3

THUNDEROUS PRAYERS THAT BRING MIRACLE AND POWER OF GOD TO QUENCH SATANIC INVASION IN YOUR LIFE.

"But the thunder of his power who can understand?" (Job 26:14)

Instructions on Fasting

- Fasting from 6am to 2 pm daily for 7 days.

or

- Praying for 7 Nights from 12 am to 3am with Fasting

or

- Fasting for those on medication 8 pm to 12 am (Please pray all-day for 7 days).

> Behold, the Lord's hand is not shortened, that it cannot save; neither his ear heavy that it cannot hear: But your iniquities have separated between you and your God, and your sins have hid his face from you, that he will not hear. For your hands are defiled with blood, and your fingers with iniquity; your lips have spoken lies, your tongue hath muttered perverseness. (Isaiah 59:1-3)

Fasting and Prayer

Confess your sins and sins of your fathers and mothers knowingly or unknowingly.

1. Thank God for his mercies and faithfulness upon your life.
2. Worship in his presence with songs and hymn of your choice.
3. Shout! Oh God, guard my spirit man while entering into this praying and fasting programme in Jesus name Amen.
4. My prayer and fasting will not be in vain in Jesus name Amen.
5. Oh Lord, unclutter my spiritual pipe from the desires of the flesh, in Jesus name Amen (Romans 8 v 6).
6. God of Abraham, Isaac, and Jacob, speak in my condition in Jesus name, Amen.
7. The Kingdom of God, break in pieces and consume every kingdom working against me as I go into this prayer in Jesus name Amen.

> And in the days of these kings shall the God of heaven set up a kingdom, which

shall never be destroyed: and the
kingdom shall not be left to other people,
but it shall break in pieces and consume
all these kingdoms, and it shall stand
forever.

(Daniel 2:44 KJV)

8. Oh Lord, deliver me from lions' mouth in Jesus name Amen.
9. Every Barrier to my breakthrough, break in pieces in Jesus name, Amen.
10. Whatever power that has decided to cut me off from God, be crushed in Jesus Name Amen. (2 Chronicle 26:21)
11. I refuse to be weak in the spirit in Jesus name. (Isaiah 14:10)
12. Any power pursing me to be weak in my faith, die in Jesus name, Amen.
13. Any power that is assigned against the knowledge of God in my life, perish in Jesus Name, Amen. (2 Corinthians 10:8-13.)
14. Oh Lord, cease the power of my oppressors in Jesus name, Amen. (Isaiah 14 verse 4)
15. Problems mocking my prayers and situation, catch fire in Jesus name, Amen.
16. Every yoke chasing away my destiny helpers break in Jesus name Amen. (Mathew 20 verse 29 -34)
17. Mysterious hands and powers holding my destiny, be roasted to ashes in Jesus name, Amen.
18. Any problem of many years in my life, expire now in Jesus name, Amen.
19. Any bullet of the wicked man targeted at me and my family, backfire in Jesus mighty name, Amen.
20. Every work of the enemy in my life, expire now in Jesus name, Amen.
21. Tempter of my life, receive the judgement of God in Jesus name, Amen.
22. Jesus help me to unclutter sin that has over-powered my life in Jesus name, Amen. (1 Peter 5:7) Cast all your anxiety on him because he cares for you.
23. Angels of success and power, locate me and my family now in Jesus name, Amen.

4

PRAYER FOR STRENGTH

Psalms 37:4 -17, Proverbs 9:10, Roman 12 :1, Galatians 2:20, Luke 9:23-24

"But the salvation of the righteous is of the Lord: he is their strength in the time of trouble" (Psalms 37:39)

"As long as Uzziah sought the Lord, God made him prosper" (2 Chronicles 26:5)

1. Thank God for another day to be in his presence.
2. Thank God for his presence in your life.
3. Thank God for strengthening your faith and power to take him at his word.
4. I submit myself to you Jesus, take over, my heavenly Father, in Jesus name Amen.
5. I surrender my all to you oh Lord, my life I surrender to you, take over Jehovah in Jesus name, Amen.
6. Forgive me my sins oh Lord, I take my hands off all my problems, I surrender all to you take over, in Jesus name, Amen. (Mark 10:27-30) For with God all things are possible.
7. Oh Lord, I offer my body, soul, and spirit as a living sacrifice, holy and pleasing to God, fight my unknown and unseen battles in Jesus name, Amen.
8. I cover myself and family with the blood of Jesus.
9. I repurchase my body, soul and spirit with the blood of Jesus.
10. I repurchase my family with the blood of Jesus.
11. I repurchase my ministry with the blood of Jesus.
12. I repurchase my calling with the blood of Jesus.
13. I repurchase my job, my business with the blood of Jesus Christ.
14. I repurchase my health with the blood of Jesus Christ, Amen.
15. I repurchase my children with the blood of Jesus Christ, Amen.
16. I repurchase my foundation with the blood of Jesus. (Psalms 11:3)
17. I hide my testimony in the blood of Jesus Christ, Amen.
18. Oh Lord, help me as I fix my eyes on you in Jesus name, Amen.
"But my eyes are fixed on you, Sovereign Lord; In you I take refuge; Do not give me over to death" (Psalms   141:8)
19. Thank you Jesus for my deliverance.

5

GREATNESS

Greatness is the manifestation of Christ nature to the people of the world, by reaching out to the needy, imparting God's goodness to those around you, your family, people in the community, building people, saving lives, manifesting God's given gift, prospering in your career, your health, your calling as a prophet of God, your academic, your finances, and being a carrier of God's presence and anointing like Moses. Daniel and Joseph prospered in their own time and were recorded as great obedient servants of God.

> Thine, O Lord is the greatness, and the power, and the glory, and the victory, and the majesty: for all that is in the heaven and in the earth is thine; thine is the kingdom, O Lord, and thou art exalted as head above all (1 Chronicles 29:11).

Greatness does not come from self-destruction, rather from your service to humanity and obedience to God's word. The word of God teaches you how your service to God will gradually build towards greatness and also gives you the power to destroy the powers opposing your greatness, through prayers, God's word, faith and wisdom from God. Everything written about God is great, there is no smallness in God. *"For great is the LORD, and greatly to be praised: he also is to be feared above all gods."* 1 Chronicles 16:25

Therefore, take a challenge to become great or face a challenge to become great through Christ Jesus. Don't lose hope when you face challenges, rather apply the faith you have in Christ Jesus through his word.

You are born to fight and win, God has embedded greatness in you, don't allow laziness, opposition, offenders, and naysayers (critics) to stop your drive to greatness. Always focus on God's word and its potentials, forget about your limitations. The scripture tells us that *"…from the days of John the Baptist until now the kingdom of heaven suffereth violence, and the violent take it by force"* (Mathew 11:12 KJV). However, this violence does not indicate mere physical fight, but most importantly include spiritual fight. You need to pray very hard to combat the spiritual war in the realm of the spirit.

King Solomon was greater in riches and wisdom than all the other kings of the earth. (1Kings 10:23) Read 1Kings 4:29-34.

For the readers of this God-inspired prayer book, greatness means that you will operate above principality and powers and rulers of this world, you will only be above not beneath. Whatever you are doing, do it with passion, commitment and use your God-given gift. *"Every good gift and every perfect gift is from above, and cometh down from the Father of lights, with whom is no variableness, neither shadow of turning"* (James 1:17)

RULES FOR GREATNESS
1. Ask God for your vision and integrity (Solomon Asked God for wisdom 1Kings 2:1-4, 10-12.)
2. Discover and grow your vision and dreams.
3. Don't discuss your vision and dreams with people who will kill your dreams. (Proverbs 23:9.)
4. Never think small. (Psalms 24:1, God, which is your heavenly father, owns the earth)
5. Ignore negative people and never listen to naysayers.
6. Always pursue your vision with wisdom and put more efforts to understand the times and season you are in, for in the middle of difficulty lies opportunities.
7. God is the root of greatness, always abide with God in all issues of life.
8. Surrender your life to Christ, operate and allow the Holy Spirit to direct you in your daily affairs
9. Being a born-again is a must for you to operate in God's given success and greatness. (Proverbs 10:22) *"The blessings of the Lord make rich and add no sorrow"*.
10. Write down your vision and run with it.
11. You need to ask God for empowerment.
12. You need the presence of God.
13. You need to trust wholly in God.
14. You need to have faith in God.
15. Ask God to teach you time and season you are in, in Jesus name Amen. (Ephesians 5:16).
16. Refrain from sin (Sin can be a blockage to your greatness).
17. Information - you need knowledge from both God and man.
18. Breaking the barriers of disappointment using God's word.

19. Breaking the flow of witchcraft, faithlessness, hatreds and envy using God's word.
20. Receiving first-hand information from the Lord (Hearing God's Voice)
21. Becoming what God says you will be. (Deuteronomy 28:1-14)
22. Do not envy sinners. (Proverbs 23:17)
23. Avoid strange men and women who are set to pull you down. (Proverbs 23:28).
24. Pray without ceasing. (1 Thessalonians 5:16-18).
25. Operating in endless testimony.

PRAYERS FOR GREATNESS.

Confession:

I am what God said I am

I am created in God's image,

I share and remain part and parcel of God's DNA,

I am a partaker of God's Covenant,

I will be above only, in Jesus name Amen.

My Greatness will not and cannot be hindered by any form of opposition.

"But seek ye first the kingdom of God, and his righteousness; and all these things shall be added unto you." Mathew 6:33

Prayers

1. Oh God, have mercy on me and my family, forgive me my sins in Jesus name, Amen.
2. Powers of darkness present in this prayer meeting to swallow my prayers lose your hold, break and rise no more in Jesus name, Amen.
3. I take authority in my dream by the power in the blood of Jesus Christ, Amen.
4. I untie myself from the hands of satanic powers in Jesus name Amen.
5. My vision and dream for GREATNESS, receive power, in Jesus name Amen.
6. Anoint me with your holy oil oh Lord, in Jesus name Amen
7. Anoint me with oil of greatness in Jesus name, Amen.
8. Shout it loud! I will see the glory of God and his greatness in my life from today in Jesus name, Amen. "But Peter and they that were with him were heavy with sleep: and when they were awake, they see his glory and the two men that stood with him". (Luke 9:32)
9. I will see God's kingdom and his greatness while I am alive on earth, in Jesus name Amen.
10. Power of deliverance, locate me now in Jesus name, Amen. (Mathew 16:19).

11. Power to discover my God-given vision and dream, locate me now in Jesus name Amen.
12. Wisdom from God, possess me now as it happened to Solomon in the bible, in Jesus name, Amen.
13. Any power set to slow me down on my road to greatness, perish now, in Jesus name Amen. (Nehemiah 4:7-9)
14. Any power set to slow me down on my road to success, perish now, in Jesus name Amen.
15. Any personality, power, ancestral spirit that has occupied my greatness, come out now and perish, in Jesus name, Amen.
16. Oh God, show me the way to my greatness, in Jesus name Amen. (Genesis 28:10-19)
17. Oh God of heaven and earth, reveal to me the hidden plan behind the enemy of my greatness, in Jesus name, Amen.
18. Oh Lord God of host, destroy the enemy of my greatness, in Jesus name, Amen.
19. Lion of Judah, arise and change my life for the best according to your word which says, I will do a new thing in your life. (Isaiah 43:19, Deuteronomy 30:9)
20. Every delay to my greatness, be cancelled in Jesus name, Amen
21. Sing praises to God who answers prayer.
22. Every information, wisdom, hidden to the advancement of my greatness, locate me now, be released unto me now. (Luke 9:45).
23. Every information I need for my greatness, be released onto me now, in Jesus name, Amen (Jeremiah 33:3.)
24. Every witchcraft power over my greatness and success, be destroyed in Jesus name, Amen
25. Fear of Greatness in my life, break in Jesus mighty name, Amen.
26. Every comfort zone in my life that prevents my greatness, be destroyed in Jesus name, Amen.
27. Arrow of selfishness preventing my greatness, backfire in Jesus name, Amen.
28. Arrow of anger preventing my greatness, backfire in Jesus name, Amen.
29. Arrow of pretense set to pull down my greatness, backfire in Jesus name, Amen.
30. Arrow of addiction pulling down my greatness and success, backfire in Jesus name, Amen.
31. Arrow of jealousy pulling down my greatness and success, backfire in Jesus name, Amen.
32. Any power that has imprisoned my greatness, break in Jesus name, Amen.
33. Spiritual imprisonment dedicated to stop my promotion in life, break in Jesus name, Amen.

34. Oh Lord, forgive me for stealing someone else's knowledge and idea which has affected my greatness in Jesus name Amen.
35. Thank you Jesus for answering my prayers in Jesus name Amen.

6

DEALING WITH THE POWERS THAT SHUT THE WINDOWS OF YOUR GREATNESS, CALLING AND DESTINY.

When you have a revelation, vision, dreams and words of knowledge, which speaks upliftment in your life, don't keep quiet by saying it is a good dream rather pray and fast until it comes to pass in your life. Same applies when you have a negative vision, dreams, and prophecy, all you need to do is to pray until negativity vanishes from your life. You are born to enjoy your freedom in Christ Jesus. (Galatians 5:13). You need access to God, your imagination cannot change the mind of God, what changes the mind of God is God's word written in the scripture. Jonah was asked to go to Nineveh but Jonah ran away from the Lord, not knowing that all power belongs to God. When the enemy of greatness has seen that Jonah could save lives in the great city of Nineveh, the voice of disobedience was unleashed in the heart of Jonah and when Jonah realised the greatness of God, he prayed from the belly of fish and God answered and saved the people of Nineveh. Do not run away from your vision, your dream, the word of God, and word of knowledge, for your greatness is now.

PRAYERS

1. Food sent from the kingdom of darkness to destroy my greatness, back to your sender in Jesus name, Amen. (Proverbs 23:1-3)
2. Food eaten in the dream to pollute my greatness, be destroyed in Jesus name, Amen.
3. Blood of Jesus, purge out all food I ate in the dream from the day I was born until today in Jesus name, Amen.
4. Any dream that has destroyed my greatness, be reversed now, in Jesus name, Amen.
5. I reject every satanic discussion in my dream, in Jesus name, Amen. (Proverbs 23:7).
6. I vomit every evil food I ate in the dream, in Jesus name, Amen. (Proverbs 23:8).
7. Oh Lord, bring to an end powers tormenting me in the dream, in Jesus name, Amen. (Proverbs 23 v 18).
8. Oh Lord, cut off from my life, strange men and women who are set to pull me down physically and spiritually, in Jesus name, Amen. (Proverbs 23:28 KJV).
9. The fire of God enter into my body, uproot all evil deposits and destroy the depositors in Jesus name Amen.

10. Blood of Jesus, uproot every sickness that is limiting my greatness and destiny in Jesus name Amen.
11. Powers of darkness controlling my life, expire now in Jesus name, Amen.
12. I break powers programmed to stop my greatness, in Jesus name, Amen.
13. Networking powers of witches and wizards fighting my greatness, be destroyed in Jesus name, Amen
14. Oh Lord, fight my battle in Jesus name, Amen.
15. Marine powers holding my greatness, break now and forever in Jesus name, Amen. (Isaiah 30:27)
16. Marine powers from my foundation fighting my greatness and destiny, be broken with the blood of Jesus, in Jesus name, Amen.
17. Thunder voice of God, enter into my life and uproot demonic powers hindering my greatness.
18. Thunder voice of God, enter into my life and uproot demonic powers hindering my business.
19. Thunder voice of God, enter into my life and uproot demonic powers hindering my fruitfulness.
20. Thunder voice of God, enter into my life and uproot demonic powers hindering my job.
21. Thunder voice of God, enter into my life and uproot demonic powers hindering my financial breakthrough in Jesus name, Amen.
22. Thunder voice of God, enter into my life and break marine powers tormenting my life in Jesus name, Amen. (Isaiah 30:27).
23. My destiny, greatness and health that are hidden in the ocean, sea, waters, rivers, lake, be vomited by the power in the blood of Jesus Christ, Amen and Amen. (Job 20:15)
24. I will not labour in vain, in Jesus name, Amen. (Psalms 104:23)
25. Stronghold of failure fashioned against my destiny and next level, break in Jesus name, Amen.
26. Riches of God on earth orchestrated to catapult my life, my destiny into divine greatness, be released onto me now in Jesus name, Amen. (Psalms 104:24) .
27. Spirit of God, speak into my destiny in Jesus name, Amen. "And thine ears shall hear a word behind thee, saying, this is the way, walk ye in it, when ye turn to the right hand, and when ye turn to the left." (Isaiah 30:21)
29. Any seed, offerings, tithes, I have sown in wrong altar that is working against my destiny and greatness, be terminated, cease your operation in my life by the power in the blood of Jesus Christ, Amen. (Isaiah 30:6).
30. Sickness programmed to end my life, cease your operation in my body now, in Jesus name, Amen.

31. Peace of God that passes all understanding, enter and overshadow my life, in Jesus name, Amen (Philippians 4:6-7, John 16:33).
32. Oh God, give me a new song of victory in Jesus name, Amen (Isaiah 30:29)
33. My Hidden blessing, manifest now in Jesus name, Amen.
34. Spirit of failure in my bloodline saying no to my greatness, be broken in Jesus name, Amen. (Lamentation 5:16)
35. My fallen glory, arise and fall no more in Jesus name, Amen.
36. My fallen destiny, arise and fall no more in Jesus name, Amen.
37. My fallen success, arise and fall no more in Jesus name, Amen.
38. Oh God, deliver me from anything that destroys prosperity and greatness in Jesus name, Amen.
39. Oh Lord, save me from witches and wizards that destroy prosperity and greatness in Jesus name, Amen.
40. I detach my life and family from powers of failure operating in my foundation with the blood of Jesus, Amen.
41. I attach my life and family to the blood of Jesus Christ, Amen.
42. God of favour, come upon my life, favour me now in Jesus name, Amen.
43. I recover my destiny from evil diversion, in Jesus name, Amen.
44. Thank God for these prayers in Jesus name, Amen.

7

PRAYER AGAINST ENEMIES OF YOUR LIFE

1. Every arrow of marital loss, I am not your candidate lose your hold from my marriage now in Jesus name, Amen.
2. Problems set to disgrace me, bow now, hear the word of the Lord and perish in Jesus name, Amen.
3. Blood of Jesus paralyse every evil personality attacking the source of my bread, oil in my head in Jesus name Amen.
4. Dark powers will not waste me and members of my family, in Jesus name, Amen
5. Spiritual Husband in my life be crushed in Jesus name, Amen
6. Spiritual wife in my life be crushed in Jesus name, Amen.
7. Powers caging my destiny, break and release my destiny in Jesus name, Amen.
8. Arrows fired into my destiny when I was in my mother's womb, be uprooted and go back to your sender in Jesus name, Amen.
9. Spirit of masturbation troubling my destiny, crush to pieces in Jesus name, Amen.
10. Any idol in my life is destroyed in Jesus name, Amen.
11. Powers feeding me in the dream, roast to ashes in Jesus name, Amen.
12. Disarm my enemies oh Lord, in Jesus mighty name, Amen.
13. Break the hands of my enemies oh Lord, in Jesus name, Amen.
14. Any backbone of the enemy saying no to my testimony, break in Jesus name, Amen.
15. Oh Lord remove any negative energy from my life, in Jesus name, Amen.
16. Powers of darkness swallowing my prayer, vomit them now in Jesus name, Amen.
17. I take territories in my dreams in Jesus name, Amen.
18. Satanic lion rising against my promotion, die in Jesus name, Amen.
19. Oh Lord, subdue my enemies in Jesus name, Amen (Psalms 47:3)
20. Every external and internal enemy fighting my destiny, be destroyed in Jesus name, Amen.
21. Powers arranging bullets against my head, be broken in Jesus name Amen. (1 Peter 4:11)
22. Every blood-drinking demon operating in my life, be crushed in Jesus name, Amen.

23. Any man, woman, power, blocking the gate of my breakthrough, be destroyed in Jesus name, Amen.

24. Negative voices speaking over my life and promotion, be silenced in Jesus name, Amen.

25. Oh Lord, end adversaries blocking my open door, in Jesus name, Amen. (Psalms 7:6).

26. Oh Lord, reduce the enemies of my life to nothing in Jesus name, Amen.

27. Any power in the world working against God's promises in my life break in Jesus Amen. (1John 4:4).

28. Oh Lord, lift me high from anywhere the enemy has buried me and my blessing in Jesus name, Amen.

29. Powers that hate my existence, your time is up, therefore, die in Jesus name, Amen.

30. Anyone using day and night to attack me, die in Jesus name, Amen.

31. All those gathered to kill me suddenly over my property and success, receive destruction and die in Jesus name Amen.

32. I jump out from every satanic bus stop in Jesus name, Amen.

33. Any power that wants to give me fake glory, be destroyed in Jesus name, Amen.

34. My Clothe in the custody of witches, catch fire in Jesus name, Amen.

35. Blood of Jesus, unwrap evil rope used by the enemy to tie me, in Jesus name, Amen.

36. Spirit of God, destroy spiritual husband operation in my body in Jesus name, Amen.

37. Oh Lord, break and destroy the foundations of witchcraft in my life in Jesus name, Amen. (Acts 16:26).

38. Dominion mandate of God's protection and blessing overshadow my family in Jesus name, Amen.

39. Agent of sickness in my life and family, die in Jesus name, Amen.

40. Blood of Jesus, protect me and my family in Jesus name, Amen.

8

PRAYER ON HIGH PLACES

"I will destroy your high places, cut down your incense altars and pile your dead bodies[b] on the lifeless forms of your idols, and I will abhor you."

(Leviticus 26:30)

Dealing with high places can be tough and seems physically impossible but when you involve Christ Jesus, God his father the owner of your life, the maker of the universe and his angels, you will see God going into the high places to fight your battles.

Let me share the testimony of how God delivered me from spiritual husband. One night the spiritual husband slept on my bed with me and I didn't know. In the morning by 6 am, an image walked out from my bed and slammed the door, I was in shock seeing such activity while I was single and not married as at that time. When I woke up, I discovered that my door was locked, I asked myself how did this man come into my room? I was completely annoyed and began to pray, then God opened my eyes and said to me that it came from the high places. And that all I need to do is to dismantle its house in a high place. Immediately, I started praying on high places that my enemies occupy. Having done that prayer, the visitation of the spiritual husband stopped because I have destroyed its abode, glory be to God. It is now your time to take authority over high places. Pray with anger in your spirit to release your miracle from high places and crush the custodians.

The Lord God is my strength, And He has made my feet like hinds' feet And makes me walk on my high places. For the choir director, on my stringed instruments (Habakkuk 3:19)

PRAYERS
1. I cover myself with the blood of Jesus Christ, Amen
2. High places harbouring my destiny, release it now in Jesus name, Amen.
3. High places controlling my life, be destroyed in Jesus name, Amen.

4. Power of high places will not kill me in Jesus name, Amen. (2 Samuel 1:19).
5. Power of High places frustrating my job, break and die in Jesus name, Amen.
6. Powers of the high place frustrating my marriage die in Jesus name, Amen.
7. Oh Lord, walk into the high places of the enemies of my life and crush their plans over my marriage, fruitfulness, documentation and ministry in Jesus name, Amen. (Amos 4:13).
8. High places of witchcraft I have stepped into with my feet to offer sacrifices to the god's, I denounce my covenant with you now, in Jesus name, Amen. (Ezekiel 20:28-29).
9. Halloween altars and witches controlling my destiny be destroyed, break off my life in Jesus name, Amen.
10. Sacrifices representing me in any altar catch fire, be roasted to ashes in Jesus name Amen.
11. I destroy the high places of spiritual husband/wife in my life in Jesus name, Amen.

"He removed the high places, and brake the images, and cut down the groves, and brake in pieces the brasen serpent that Moses had made: for unto those days the children of Israel did burn incense to it: and he called it Nehushtan (2Kings 18:4)

12. Charms, powers, acquired from satanic high places being worshipped in my house, catch fire in Jesus name, Amen.
13. I collect my honey, money, health, and all blessings hidden in the high places in Jesus name, Amen.

"He made him ride on the high places of the earth, and he ate the produce of the field; and He made him suck honey from the rock, and oil from the flinty rock." (Deuteronomy 32:13)

14. Thank you, Jesus, for the escape.

"No temptation has overtaken you except such as is common to man; but God is faithful, who will not allow you to be tempted beyond what you are able, but with the temptation will also make the way of escape, that you may be able to bear it." (1 Corinthians 10:13)

9

UNLOCKING SPIRITUAL KEYS HOLDING YOUR BREAKTHROUGHS IN BONDAGE

Key is a symbol of authority, the power to rule over everything. It also has spiritual connotation which can be used to close and open the doors of wealth, knowledge, love, happiness destiny, vision, calling and wisdom. Keys can also be used to lock adverse doors that inhibit success and promotion in life. When you dream about a key, all you need to do is to pray a controlling prayer to bring into manifestation the good things that God has given to you in the dream or vision to come to pass, and also pray a destroying prayer to destroy any power that has locked or imprisoned you and your blessing in the spiritual realm. Key is an important spiritual powerful weapon that is used in prayer to open locked doors in the spirit.

Before you start the prayers below buy a pad lock with keys. Pray all the prayers on key and padlock below for (7) seven days, and finally unlock the padlock with the key, then dispose the padlock in a separate bin and the keys in a separate bin, you'll see the lord working in your favour.

I will place on his shoulder the key to the house of David; what he opens no one can shut, and what he shuts no one can open. (Isaiah 22:22)

The Lord gave the word: great was the company of those that published it. (Psalms 68:11)

For I am the Lord your God who takes hold of your right hand "and says to you, do not fear; I will help you" (Isaiah 41 v 13)

PRAYERS

1. Powers of darkness holding the keys of my destiny release it now. Let the power be destroyed in Jesus name, Amen. And the light shines in the darkness, and the darkness did not comprehend it. (John 1:5)
2. Keys to my destiny, house, marriage, be released to me in Jesus name, Amen.
3. Any obstacle on my application to the new house be broken in Jesus, name Amen.
4. Lord with this key in my hand, I unlock my destiny from where the enemy has locked it, in Jesus name, Amen.

5. With this key, I unlock and destroy powers holding me in bondage in Jesus name Amen.
6. Oh Lord, unlock my house, my marriage, my health, from the spiritual prison holding my breakthrough in Jesus name, Amen.
7. Oh Lord God of Isaac and Jacob, arise let your hail and thunder smite and break every padlock and key used in blocking my destiny in Jesus name, Amen.
8. Oh Lord destroy every stagnating power operating in my life in Jesus name, Amen.
9. Oh Lord scatter and crush the kings and queens from marine kingdom working in my life in Jesus name (Psalms 68:14).
10. Kings and Queens from the pit of hell that have refused to let me and my family to go out of bondage, die in Jesus name, Amen. (Isaiah 6:1).
11. Oh Lord, dismantle the authority of spiritual husband and wife in my life and family in Jesus name, Amen.
12. Any power extending my problem, perish now in Jesus name, Amen.
13. Anything in my body that is connected to the kingdom of darkness, be destroyed in Jesus name, Amen.
14. Evil mark in my body that is connected to the kingdom of darkness, be dismantled and be destroyed.
15. Any satanic object moving in my body used in controlling my life, be destroyed in Jesus name, Amen.
16. Every controlling gadget used by the enemy to frustrate my life, be crushed in Jesus name.
17. You network of enemies programmed into my life to frustrate me, die in Jesus name Amen.
18. Oh Lord destroy the programming cable of darkness used to monitor my life in Jesus name.
19. With this key in my hand, I shut up every evil conspiracy, wicked powers, evil decision, that is operating in my life in Jesus name, Amen.
20. Every gang up against me in the dream, be crushed in Jesus name, Amen.
21. Every power challenging the power of God in my life and my family as I unlock this padlock, let your power be broken in Jesus name, Amen.
22. Jesus, manifest your power in this battle and give me victory over my enemies. (Psalms 21:9).
23. Oh God grant my prayer request for my new house in Jesus name, Amen.
24. Father king of glory, give me victory in this battle in Jesus name, Amen.

25. Oh Lord, use your mighty right hand to root out my problems in Jesus name, Amen (Psalms 21:8).
26. Any power holding my next level in bondage, be unlocked in the mighty name of Jesus.
27. Anywhere my testimony is locked, I unlock it in Jesus name, Amen.
28. Lord, I thank you for answering my prayers in Jesus name, Amen.
29 I cover myself with the blood of Jesus.
30. Favour of God, envelope me and my family every day of my life in Jesus name, Amen.
I pray for you to come out from the cage of the enemy in Jesus name, Amen.

10

PRAYERS ON MARRIAGE

PART 1

Therefore, as you received Christ Jesus the Lord, so walk in him, rooted and built up in him and established in the faith, just as you were taught, abounding in thanksgiving. (Colossians 2:6 – 7)

1. Thunder fire of God mixed with hail, destroy every stagnancy in my marriage in Jesus name Amen. (Exodus 9:23)
2. Satanic lock on my marriage, be broken in Jesus name, Amen
3. Powers of poverty operating in my marriage, be broken in Jesus name, Amen.
4. My marriage reject curses from my fathers and mothers house, in Jesus name Amen.
5. Curses operating in my marriage from my husband or wife's house be broken in Jesus name, Amen.
6. Hidden spiritual wicked powers operating in my marriage, be exposed be broken in Jesus names (Jeremiah 33:3).
7. Every Judgement of Darkness against my marriage, be cancelled in Jesus name Amen.
8. Every known and unknown limitations working against me, my marriage and my family, be crushed in Jesus name, Amen.
9. Every unknown limitations from my foundation be broken in Jesus name, Amen.
10. Limitation's from my aunts, uncles, cousins and family members affecting my marriage, lose your hold of me, break and be destroyed in Jesus, name Amen.
11. Any power limiting my financial breakthrough in my marriage be destroyed in Jesus name, Amen.
12. Any power limiting my future husband, future wife and future children be destroyed in Jesus name, Amen.
13. Power of sickness assigned to my marriage be destroyed in Jesus name, Amen.
14. I refuse to be controlled by evil demonic name, in Jesus name, Amen.
15. Blood of Jesus, purge out witchcraft limitation from my bloodline in Jesus name Amen.
16. Rock of Ages crush witchcraft powers limiting my destiny and marriage in Jesus name Amen.
17. Sickness attached to my marriage, die in Jesus name amen.

18. Oh God, restore my marriage from calamity in Jesus name, Amen.
19 Oh Lord, restore my marriage from strange women and men in Jesus name, Amen.
20. Envious powers operating in my marriage, break and die in Jesus name, Amen.
21. Power of hatred operating in my marriage, die in Jesus name, Amen.
22. Anyone using day and night to attack my marriage, your time is up, die in Jesus name, Amen.
23. Poison sent to destroy my marriage, go back to your sender in Jesus name, Amen.
24. Arrow of poverty sent to attack my marriage, go back to your sender in Jesus name, Amen.
25. Arrow of confusion fired into my marriage go back to your sender in Jesus name, Amen.
26. Evil pattern operating in my marriage, break in Jesus name, Amen.
27. I recover my marriage from evil diversion in Jesus name, Amen.
28. Fake glory operating in my marriage, die in Jesus name.
29. Oh Lord, remember my marriage for financial breakthrough in Jesus name, Amen.
30. Oh Lord, remove sickness from my marriage in Jesus name, Amen.
31. My marriage reject arrow of untimely death in Jesus name, Amen.
32. Marine powers controlling my marriage, break in Jesus name, Amen.
33. Powers assigned to waste all good efforts made in my marriage, die in Jesus name, Amen.
34. Covenant of childlessness in my marriage, die in Jesus name, Amen.
35. Blood of Jesus, enter into my marriage and uproot sickness, sorrow, death and poverty in Jesus name, Amen.
36. Blood of Jesus, protect my marriage in Jesus name, Amen.
37. The fire of God, be a hedge round about my marriage in Jesus name, Amen.
38. The seed of disappointment I swallowed in my dream, melt now and be flushed out of my body in Jesus name, Amen
39. Oh God, open my heaven and show me visions of my marriage in Jesus name, Amen. (Isaiah 45:11)
40. Oh Lord, lay your hand of healing on my marriage in Jesus name, Amen. (Ezekiel 1:13).

PART 2
Prayers for Marriage: Spinsters and Bachelors.
"There shall not be found among you any one that maketh his son or his daughter to pass through the fire, or that useth divination, or an observer of times, or an enchanter, or a witch." (Deuteronomy 18:10)

1. Lord, I thank you for keeping me alive in Jesus name, Amen.
2. Father king of glory, I am a sinner forgive my sins in Jesus name, Amen.
3. Receive my praise and prayer Lord Jesus Christ.
4. Power of failure dedicated against my prayer, die in Jesus name, Amen.
5. The sexual link I have with my ex-partners break in Jesus name, Amen
6. The sexual link I have with my ex-husband, break in Jesus name, Amen.
7. The sexual link I have with my ex-boyfriends, break in Jesus name, Amen.
8. The sexual link I have with my ex-girlfriend, be broken in Jesus name, Amen.
9. The serpent from marine kingdom tormenting my marriage, die in Jesus name, Amen.
10. Serpent transferred to my body preventing me from getting married, die in Jesus name, Amen.
11. Sexually transmitted diseases that are preventing me from getting married, die forever in Jesus name, Amen.
12. Food from dreams deposited in my body, melt and be flushed out of my body in Jesus name I pray, Amen.
13. Blood of Jesus Christ, wipe out evil marks on my forehead in Jesus name, Amen.
14. Spirit of "promise and fail" assigned to fight my marriage, die in Jesus name, Amen.
15. Power of disappointment in my life, be broken in Jesus name, Amen.
16. Spirit husband/wife that has married me spiritually, I divorce you today in Jesus name Amen.
17. Sperm from spirit husband inside my body melt and be flushed out with the blood of Jesus Christ, in Jesus name, Amen.
18. Fluid from spirit wife inside my body melt and be flushed out with the blood of Jesus Christ in Jesus name I pray, Amen.
19. I return all the marriage rings I collected in the dream from spiritual husband/wife by fire in Jesus name, Amen.
20. I divorce all friends I have in the waters in Jesus name, Amen.

21. The liquid fire of God burn to ashes my houses in the waters, sea, ocean and rivers in Jesus name, Amen.
22. My marriage in the waters, I divorce you today in Jesus name, Amen.
23. Thunder fire of God, strike, dismantle and destroy powers holding me in the waters in Jesus name, Amen.
24. Thunder fire of God, strike, dismantle, and destroy powers holding my marriage in the waters in Jesus name I pray, Amen.
25. Thunder fire of God, take my marriage out of the waters in Jesus name, Amen.
26. Hidden spiritual powers preventing my future husband from locating me, die in Jesus name, Amen.
27. Hidden spiritual powers preventing my future wife from locating me, die in Jesus name, Amen.
28. I cook my body, spirit, soul and mind with the blood of Jesus, I am no longer in the bondage of marine powers in Jesus name, Amen.
29. I destroy every link with marine children with the blood of Jesus Christ, Amen.
30. Marine bed, reject me by fire in Jesus name I pray, Amen.
31. Foundational powers in charge of spinsterhood and bachelorhood in my family, die in Jesus name Amen.
32. Eyes from the waters monitoring my future husband, be blinded in Jesus name I pray, Amen.
33. Eyes from the waters monitoring my future wife, be blinded in Jesus name, Amen.
34. Body odour assigned to scatter my marriage to my future husband, be wiped out with the blood of Jesus Christ, Amen.
35. Body odour assigned to scatter my marriage to my future wife, be wiped out with the blood of Jesus Christ Amen.
36. Witchcraft power from the forest resisting my marriage, die in Jesus name, Amen.
37. Family members holding my marriage in bondage, release my marriage now, in Jesus name, Amen.
38. Evil pot vomit, my marriage now in Jesus name, Amen.
39. Sea creatures that swallowed my marriage, vomit them now in Jesus name I pray, Amen. He hath swallowed down riches, and he shall vomit them up again: God shall cast them out of his belly (Job 20:15)
40. Thunder fire of God, set ablaze altars that have refused to release my marriage now in Jesus name, Amen.
41. Hammer of God, break and smash to pieces demonic clock of the enemy operating in my marriage in Jesus name, Amen. (Jeremiah 23:29).

42. Foundational limitation, your time is up, break off my life in Jesus name, Amen.

43. Agreement by my forefathers to stop me from getting married, break in Jesus name Amen. "He made the earth by his power; he founded the world by his wisdom and stretched out the heavens by his understanding. When he thunders, the waters in the heavens roar; he makes clouds rise from the ends of the earth. He sends lightning with the rain and brings out the wind from his storehouses. (Jeremiah 51: 15-16)

44. Every marriage curse operating in my life die in Jesus name, Amen.

45. Long time battle in my life die in Jesus name, Amen.

46. Chains of spinsterhood in my life be broken in Jesus name, Amen.

47. Witchcraft powers in my foundation manipulating my marriage be destroyed with the blood of Jesus Christ, Amen.

48. Anti-husband syndrome in my bloodline, die in Jesus name, Amen.

49. Anti-wife syndrome in my bloodline, die in Jesus name, Amen.

50. Soul-tie covenant with my parent frustrating my marriage, be broken in Jesus name, Amen.

51. Chains of bachelorhood in my life be broken in Jesus name, Amen.

52. My husband manifest from wherever you are hidden in the face of the earth and locate me by fire, in Jesus name, Amen.

53. My wife manifest from wherever you are hidden in the face of the earth and locate me by fire in Jesus name, Amen.

54. My foundation come out of bondage now in Jesus name.

55. Blood of Jesus, flush out the mark of hatred from my life in Jesus name, Amen.

56. Power of anger resisting my marriage to the next level, die in Jesus name, Amen.

57. Oh Lord, draw out thy sword and cut off the head of spiritual husband in my life in Jesus name, Amen.

58. Heaven over my marriage open now in Jesus name, Amen.

59. Oh, Lion of Judah, appear and deal with the cases in my marriage in Jesus name, Amen.

60. Power of regret in my marriage, break and be destroyed in Jesus name, Amen.

61. Oh Lord uproot, anything, powers, and spirits you didn't plant into my body in Jesus name, Amen. But while men slept, his enemy came and sowed tares among the wheat, and went his way. (Mathew 13:25)

62. Spirit of the Lord, destroy every concluded arrangement of the enemy in my marriage in Jesus name, Amen. "So shall they fear the name of the LORD from the west, and his glory from the rising

of the sun. When the enemy shall come in like a flood, the Spirit of the LORD shall lift up a standard against him". (Isaiah 59 v 19.)

63. The root of hardship in my marriage be uprooted in Jesus name, Amen.
64. The warehouse that is keeping my blessing be open and release my marriage in Jesus name, Amen.
65. I receive my desired husband/wife in Jesus name, Amen.
66. I receive everlasting joy and gladness from the Lord in this marriage in Jesus name Amen.
67. Spirit of God, work on my marriage and let me have an unending relationship with Jesus Christ, in Jesus name, Amen.
68. Lord Jesus envelope my marriage with favour in Jesus name, Amen.
69. My marriage receive healing in Jesus name, Amen.
70. Thank you Jesus for answering my prayers.

11

HEALING PRAYERS

1. Thank God for another day like today.
2. Oh Lord forgive me my sins in Jesus name, Amen.
3. Oh Lord have mercy on me and heal me in Jesus name, Amen.
4. You unclean spirit, come out of me now and go into bottomless pit in Jesus name, Amen.
5. Jesus, send your healing power to my body and heal this sickness in Jesus name Amen.
6. Jesus the great I am, envelope me with your healing power in Jesus name, Amen.
7. Oh Lord cleanse my life and body from witchcraft activities in Jesus name, Amen.
8. Oh Lord, let your healing arm be stretched upon my body, lift me out of dangers in Jesus name, Amen.
9. Oh Lord, unseat the strongman and woman troubling my life. (Luke 1:52)
10. Father Lord, visit this sickness with your unquenchable fire in Jesus name, Amen (Mathew 3:11-12).
11. Oh Lord, show me your great mercy over this sickness and heal me in Jesus name, Amen (Luke 1:58)
12. Oh Lord, cancel every judgement passed on me by enemies that led to this sickness, in Jesus name, Amen.
13. Oh Lord, cancel every Judgement passed on me by my foundation that led to this sickness in Jesus name, Amen.
14. Oh Lord, give me the power to trust and remain faithful in you all the days of my life in Jesus name Amen. (Psalms 23:6)
15. Oh Lord release my spirit man from the prison of familiar spirit in Jesus name, Amen.
16. Any garment of sickness I am wearing physically and spiritually be burnt to ashes, in Jesus name, Amen.
17. Every chain holding me in bondage, be broken in Jesus name, Amen.
18. I reattached my life to the blood of Jesus, in Jesus name, Amen.
19. Custodians of the evil chain in my life, be destroyed in Jesus name, Amen.
20. Custodians of sickness in my life, catch fire and be destroyed in Jesus name, Amen.
21. I receive divine immunity against all sorts of sickness and arrows, in Jesus name Amen.

22. I cancel every engagement with the spirit of death in Jesus name, Amen.
23. Any power of familiar spirit, witchcraft spirit, set to terminate my destiny be destroyed in Jesus name, Amen.
24. My time and my life is in your hand oh Lord Jesus, visit me today, deliver me from the hands of my enemies in Jesus name, Amen (Psalms 31:15).
25. My appointed time with God, manifest now in Jesus name, Amen (Ecclesiastes 3:1; 2 Corinthians 6:2)
26. This is your time of visitation in my life, Oh Lord Jesus, visit me now in Jesus name, Amen.
27. I receive power from above, for breakthrough and turn around in Jesus name, Amen.
28. I receive the power of love from above in Jesus name, Amen.
29. I receive the power of favour from above in Jesus name, Amen.
30. I receive the power of grace to overcome problems in Jesus name, Amen.
31. I receive healing from ……………….. (mention sickness) in Jesus name, Amen.
32. Diabetes, High Blood Pressure, eye problems, cancer, ulcer, chronic headache, migraine, be healed in Jesus name, Amen.
33. Father Lord, take away this sickness from me in Jesus name, Amen.
34. Lord, I thank you for healing me in Jesus name, Amen. "He sent his word, and healed them, and delivered them from their destructions". (Psalms 107:20)
35. King of glory, receive my praises in Jesus name, Amen.
36. Thank you, Jesus, for answered prayers

12

POWERS OF THE NIGHT

1. Powers that go around in the night attacking me and my family, be crushed in Jesus name, Amen.
2. Spirit husband/wife operating during the night, attacking my destiny, perish now in Jesus name, Amen
3. Witchcraft powers set to attack me in the nights, break in Jesus name, Amen.
4. Night powers that want my voice to expire, break now in Jesus name, Amen.
5. Any evil personality impersonating my God's original glory, come out of me now and perish in Jesus name, Amen.
6. Battles from my dream stagnating my life be crushed in Jesus name, Amen.
7. Oh Lord fight my night battles in Jesus name, Amen.
8. Night dreams fashioned to pull me down spiritually and physically be destroyed, Amen.
9. I dismiss the evil proposal of wicked powers in my dreams, in Jesus name, Amen.
10. Blood of Jesus, destroy every strategy used by familiar spirits to manipulate my dream in Jesus name Amen.
11. Jesus by your mercy, bring to an end powers of the night fighting me in the dream, in Jesus name, Amen. (Judges 9:52-59)
12. Oh Lord destroy night and day delicacies from demonic kingdom prepared to feed me in my dream in Jesus name, Amen.
13. Blood of Jesus, destroy the night blood drinkers and their powers in Jesus name, Amen.
14. Demonic powers using the night to attack my destiny, blood of Jesus, destroy them in Jesus name, Amen.
15. Oh Lord destroy night and day demonic delicacies offered to me in the dream in Jesus name, Amen. (Daniel 1:8).
16. Blood of Jesus, destroy all marine powers attacking me in the night and day in Jesus name, Amen.
17. Oh Lord, reveal your secret to me by night dream and vision in Jesus name (Daniel 2:19).
18. Sword of the Lord, slaughter witchcraft animals used in the night to attack me in Jesus name, Amen.
19. Wicked powers waiting to strike at an agreed time of the night be destroyed by the blood of Jesus Christ, Amen. (Psalms 37:14)

20. Powers of hatred multiplying in the night to attack me in the day time, be crushed in Jesus name, Amen.

13

THUNDER PRAYER

At this also my heart trembleth, and is moved out of his place. Hear attentively the noise of his voice, and the sound that goeth out of his mouth. He directeth it under the whole heaven and his lightning unto the ends of the earth. After it a voice roareth: he thundereth with the voice of his excellency, and he will not stay them when his voice is heard. God thundereth marvelously with his voice; great things doeth he, which we cannot comprehend. For he saith to the snow, Be thou on the earth; likewise to the small rain, and to the great rain of his strength. He sealeth up the hand of every man; that all men may know his work. (Job 37:2-7)

The brief revelation of what God told me about thunder and lightning is that both a symbolic demonstration of the power of God throughout the journey of Israelites while in Egypt. Until now thunder and lightning are powerful weapons to humble people of the world. Secondly, thunder and lightning voice out God's anger, sovereignty and punishment. They are great weapons for spiritual warfare. 1 Samuel 2:10 says "The adversaries of the Lord shall be broken to pieces; against them, he will thunder in heaven".

PRAYER

1. Thunder of God, enter into every altar where my blessing is caged now and destroy the powers holding my breakthrough in Jesus name.
2. Thunder of God, locate my hidden husband, I am ripe for marriage in Jesus name, Amen.
3. The thunder of God, locate my hidden wife, I am ready for marriage in Jesus mighty name, Amen.
4. Thunder fire of God, set ablaze altars that have refused to release my money now in Jesus name, Amen.

5. Thunder fire of God, break every known and unknown soul-tie covenant power and operations working in my life in Jesus name, Amen.
6. Thunder fire of God, appear in all the altars that collected my clothing, and destroy their authority over my life in Jesus name.
7. Thunder fire of God, enter into occultic altars, uproot all my originals and caged destinies of me and my family in Jesus name, Amen.
8. Thunder of God, strike every stagnation in my life, break and lose me from afflictions in Jesus name, Amen.
9. Thunder of God, open my doors of breakthrough and overflowing blessings in Jesus name, Amen.
10. Thunder of God, strike witchcraft foundational powers holding my marriage and greatness in Jesus name, Amen.

14

PROPHETIC BLESSING

Receive it with faith in Jesus name Amen.

1. Your lost hope is restored now in Jesus name, Amen.
2. I prophesy that what God has said about your life will send your problems into exile in Jesus name, Amen (Psalms 33:11).
3. Your divorce is cancelled and marriage restored in Jesus name, Amen.
4. That loneliness is over in Jesus name, Amen.
5. Rare sickness is destroyed in Jesus name, Amen.
6. Receive your visa now in Jesus name, Amen.
7. Receive your document in Australia, UK, US and all over the world in Jesus name, Amen.
8. Receive your pregnancy now in Jesus name, Amen.
9. Receive an unending relationship with Jesus, Amen.
10. Receive Holy Spirit now in Jesus name, Amen. (Mark 1:8).
12. You will no longer experience dryness of pocket in Jesus name, Amen.
13. You will no longer experience dryness in your spiritual life.
14. My Intimacy with God cannot be broken up in Jesus name, Amen.
15. Let the weak say I am strong in Jesus name, Amen.

PRAYER FOR BLESSING AND FAVOUR

1. Oh God locate me with genuine people who will move my destiny forward in Jesus name, Amen.
2. I step into my victory, no going back in Jesus name, Amen.
3. King of glory, manifest your glory in my life in Jesus name, Amen. (John 13:31)
4. In the battle of my life, show me your glory Jehovah, in Jesus name, Amen.
5. My blessing directed to the coven, come out and locate me in Jesus name, Amen.
6. Father, bless me with all spiritual blessings in Jesus name, Amen. (Ephesians 1:3)
7. I receive the power of the promises of God in Jesus name, Amen. (Psalms 119:89)
8. Oh Lord prepare my helpers to locate me in Jesus name, Amen.
9. I receive the power of the Holy Ghost to move my life forward in Jesus name, Amen.

10. I receive open doors to a financial breakthrough in Jesus name, Amen.
11. I receive protection from the blood of Jesus Christ, Amen.
12. I cancel the power of accident in Jesus name, Amen.
13. I receive long life and good health for the rest of my life in Jesus name, Amen.
14. Unending favour of God, embrace me now in Jesus name, Amen.
15. Laughter that has ceased in my life, be revived now in my life, in Jesus name, Amen. (Job 8:21)

BEFORE YOU DROP THIS BOOK
Ominipotent and Ominipresence God, you are worthy of my praise, I thank you for your faithfulness and answered prayers in Jesus name.

Follow up

Communicate us with your dreams and testimony on the email provided below.
Email: covenant_prophetic@yahoo.com

Feel free to join us weekly on
Facebook @ covenant prophetic prayer ministry

Youtube
https://www.youtube.com/channel/UCmB1toF1kd_zYJLgNwOLP2g/featured?view_as=subscriber

The Author
Evangelist Mrs Chidinma Anokwute is by God's Grace the founder of Covenant Prophetic Prayer Ministry in Dublin Ireland since January 2017 touching lives through the Facebook online prophetic hour, changing lives and winning souls for the kingdom of God through her prophetic gift.
Evangelist Chidinma grew up in a Christian home attended first Century Gospel church (Known as Faith Tabernacle) family church, was a member of NIFES from 1997 to 2000, Joined MFM from 2001 to date, and actively serving in Covenant prophetic prayer ministry.
She is a graduate of BED- Accounting from the University of Nigeria Nsukka, IT Carlow -Professional social Studies Ireland, MBA- Australian Business School.
She is happily married.